THIS IS
Hawai'i

THIS IS
Hawai'i
Visions of the Islands

THIS IS
Hawai'i

Visions of the Islands

. . . .

Photography by
Douglas Peebles

Library of Congress Catalog Card
Number: 2002101793

ISBN 1-56647-558-9

Photo on page 1: Heliconia; page 2-3: Pu'uhonua O Honaunau, Island of
Hawai'i; page 4-5: Ko'olina, Island of O'ahu; this page: Kalalau Beach, Island of
Kaua'i

First Printing, October 2002
1 2 3 4 5 6 7 8 9

All photos © by Douglas Peebles
Designed by Jane Hopkins

Mutual Publishing
1215 Center Street, Suite 210
Honolulu, Hawaii 96816
Ph: (808) 732-1709
Fax: (808) 734-4094
e-mail: mutual@lava.net
www.mutualpublishing.com

Printed in Korea

14 *Diamond Head, Waikīkī, on the Island of Oʻahu*

FROM THE
Sky

Kalalau Beach, Island of Kaua'i

No alien land in all the world has any
deep, strong charm for me but that one; no other land
could so longingly and so beseechingly haunt me sleeping and
waking, through half a lifetime, as that one has done. Other
things leave me, but it abides; other things change, but it remains
the same. For me its balmy airs are always blowing, its summer
seas flashing in the sun, the pulsing of its surf-beat is in my ear; I
can see its garlanded crags, its leaping cascades, its plumy palms
drowsing by the shore, its remote summits floating like
islands above the cloud rack; I can feel the spirit
of its woodland solitude, I can hear the plash of its
brooks; in my nostrils still lives the breath of flowers
that perished twenty years ago.

—*Mark Twain: Letters from the Sandwich Islands, Vol. I, Joan Abramson*

Napili Beach, Island of Maui

and Jack London wrapped phrases around the wonder that pulses like a lover's heartbeat through these islands. And still, the luminescence of the place begs for more.

This is Hawai'i blends the photographic talent of Douglas Peebles with the work of ancient chanters and literary giants, in a presentation keepsake, a photo album of images and words to entreat the senses and stimulate memories.

E komo mai a Hawai'i nei, welcome to beautiful Hawai'i. May you gather many *hali'a aloha* (cherished memories) and may your journey here fill your heart with *ka malama* (the light) of the Islands.

Note:
In the past, written Hawaiian language did not use macrons and glottal stops. The practice is generally accepted today as an aid to proper pronunciation and spelling. Diacritical markings as found in *Place Names of Hawaii* and in Pukui and Elbert's *Hawaiian Dictionary* have been added where appropriate.

Waikīkī Beach, Island o...

Introduction

Hawai'i's profound beauty transforms light into poetry. The play of clouds above the Ko'olau cliffs, the vivid reds and golds of wild flowers blooming along winding mountain trails, and the dance of shattered sunlight on rippling waves—all this spectacle demands description.

So·it was that the Islands' first people created chants telling of the winds that swirled from beach to summit and back again, and the temperamental moods of the ocean. Hawaiians gave names to the various rains that sprinkled and pounded the valleys and headlands. Through the metaphor of nature's drama, human passion for the land became enlivened and personified.

Later, other people arrived from foreign lands and used their own words to evoke the detail of what they experienced here. Robert Louis Stevenson, Mark Twain,

Nani Lēʻahi, he maka no Kahiki.

Beautiful Lēʻahi, object of the eyes
from Kahiki.

*(Diamond Head, always observed with interest
by visitors from foreign lands.)*

—Hawaiian Proverb, *ʻŌlelo Noʻeau Hawaiian
Proverbs & Poetical Sayings,* 1983

Hualālai Mountain, Island of Hawai'i

The far head of Kalalau Valley had been well chosen as a refuge. Except Kiloliana, who knew back trails up the precipitous walls, no man would win to the gorge save by advancing across a knife-edged ridge...Koolau had been driven to this refuge from the lower valley by the beach. And if he were driven from it in turn, he knew of gorges among the jumbled peaks of the inner fastnesses where he could lead his subjects and live.

—Jack London,
Koolau, the Leper, ca.1912

Kalalau Lookout, Kōke'e, Island of Kaua'i

Lahaina, Island of Maui

"Haleakalā!" cried he, triumphantly,

for he saw he had a thing or two worth showing,

a glimpse of which might content me with this world,

dull as I found it just then. "Haleakalā—the House

of the Sun–up before us," said Kahele.

"And to get into the Sun's House?"

"Make a good climb up, and go in from the top!"

Ha! to creep up the roof and drop in at the skylight: this

were indeed a royal adventure. "How long would it take?"

Kahele waxed eloquent. That night we should sleep a little

up on the slope of the mountain…in the morning

we should surprise the sun in the

turrets of his temple…

—Charles Warren Stoddard,
The House of the Sun

Haleakalā, Island of Maui

Limahuli Gardens, Island of Kaua'i   25

Hilo, Island of Hawai'i

Kalaupapa has been dramatized and fictionalized until it is known all over the world today as a spot of veiled mysticism, a cursed place where men are banished to await death and a place where martyrs sacrifice their lives in a beautiful attenuation of human suffering.

—Ernie Pyle,
Honolulu Advertiser, 1937

Kalaupapa, Island of Moloka'i

Hanauma Bay, Island of O'ahu

FROM THE

Sea

West Maui Mountains, Island of Maui

The name of
the cave was
Anaopuhi, the
cave of the eel.
Here dwelt the
great shark god
Kauhuhu and his
guardians or
watchers, Waka
and Mo-o, the
great dragons or
reptiles of
Polynesian
legends.

—W. D. Westervelt,
*Kauhuhu, the Shark God
of Molokai*, 1912

North Shore, Island of Moloka'i

Kauai from the sea, is green and rose: the bright volcanic earth showing through the rich vegetation which has caused its inhabitants to claim for it the name given to an unidentified island somewhere in these seas by an early Spanish navigator: the Garden Island.

—Clifford Gessler,
Hawaii: Isles of Enchantment, 1938

Puha ka honu, ua awakea.

When the turtle comes up
to breathe, it is daylight.

(Said when a person yawns.
Sleeping time is over; work begins.)

—Hawaiian Proverb, *'Olelo No'eau*
Hawaiian Proverbs & Poetical Sayings, 1983.

Sea Turtle

Sailboats off Waikīkī Beach, Island of Oʻahu

'Au i ke kai me he
manu ala.

Cross the sea
as a bird.

(To sail across
the sea.)

—Hawaiian Proverb,
*'Ōlelo No'eau Hawaiian
Proverbs & Poetical Sayings,*
1983

Hāmākua Coast, Island of Hawai'i

We jogged on again till we met a native who told us that we were quite close to our destination; but there were no signs of it, for we were still on the lofty uplands, and the only prominent objects were huge headlands confronting the sea.

—Isabella Bird,
*Two Hawaiian Households
on the Hamakua Coast*

A DAY AT THE

Beach

Lanika'i Beach, Island of O'ahu

Poʻipū Beach, Island of Kauaʻi

Hāpuna Beach, Kohala Coast, Island of Hawai'i   49

Ku mai, ku mai ka nalu nui, mai Kahiki mai,

popoʻi kai uli kai koʻo la.

Stand up, stand up, the big wave from Kahiki; break the

dark wave, the rough wave!

—Henry P. Judd, *Hawaiian
Proverbs and Riddles*, 1930

Wave off Waimea Bay, Island of O'ahu

Mākena Beach, Island of Maui

A leisurely pace and warm aloha still characterize the 'friendly island.' Everything moves more slowly here. You get the feeling that everyone of Moloka'i's 5,000 or so residents knows everyone else on the island.

—From the *Skies of Paradise: Hawaii*, 1990.

Kepuhi Beach, Island of Moloka‘i

WATER
Falls

Hāmākua Coast, Island of Hawaiʻi

Few even of island residents have trodden
the upper forests of Waiʻaleʻale. That great wet roof,
only a few miles from motor roads and electric power and
the sugar fields that live by its waters, remains virtually
unexplored—a legendary place, populated, according to
report, by wild swine, equally fierce wild cattle, and survi-
vors of bright birds from whose feathers Hawaiians
of old made helmets and mantles
for their chiefs.

—Clifford Gessler,
Waiʻaleʻale & Beyond, 1938

Mount Wai'ale'ale, Island of Kaua'i

Wailua Falls, Hāna Coast, Island of Maui

O Hana ua lani
ha'aha'a, ka 'āina a
ka ia iki i noho ai,
he i'a na Ku'ula
ma lāua o 'Ai'ai.

Hana of the low-
lying rain cloud,
the land where
the small fish is,
the fish of the fish
god Ku'ula and
'Ai'ai.

—Henry P. Judd,
*Hawaiian Proverbs
and Riddles*, 1930

Seven Pools, Hāna Coast, Island of Maui   65

Waimea Canyon, Island of Kaua'i

RISING

Peaks

. . . .

Napelepele na pali o Kalalau, i ka wili 'ia e ka makani.

Crumbling are the cliffs of Kalalau, twisted by the winds.

—Henry P. Judd, *Hawaiian Proverbs and Riddles*, 1930

Kalalau Valley, Island of Kaua'i

Ko'olau Mountains, Island of O'ahu

Mount Wai'ale'ale, Island of Kaua'i

E wili Koʻolau ua
ahiahi.

Twist Koʻolau, it is
evening.

—Henry P. Judd,
*Hawaiian Proverbs
and Riddles,* 1930

Ko'olau Mountains, Island of O'ahu

Molokini Islet, Island of Maui

LONE

Islands

· · · · · · ·

Chinaman's Hat, Island of Oʻahu

Ke kai leo nui o Mokoliʻi.

The loud-voiced sea of Mokoliʻi.

—Hawaiian Proverb, *ʻŌlelo Noʻeau*
Hawaiian Proverbs & Poetical Sayings, 1983

'Ālau Island, Hana Coast, Island of Maui

FIRE AND Sky

Kīlauea Volcano, Island of Hawaiʻi

It is said in the legends that "when great clouds gather on the mountains and a rainbow spans the valley, look out for furious storms of wind and rain which come suddenly, sweeping down the valley."

—W. D. Westervelt,
*Myths and Legends of
Hawaii* 1913

Coconut Palm

Kīlauea Volcano, Island of Hawai'i

Mai ka lā hiki a ka lā kau.

From the sun's arrival to the sun's rest.

*(Said of a day, from sunrise to sunset.
This phrase is much used in prayers.)*

—Hawaiian Proverb, ʻŌlelo Noʻeau
Hawaiian Proverbs & Poetical Sayings, 1983

Kāneʻohe Bay, Island of Oʻahu

The atmosphere was poisoned with
sulphurous vapors and choked with falling ashes,
pumice stones and cinders; countless columns of smoke
rose up and blended together in a tumbled canopy that hid
the heavens and glowed with a ruddy flush reflected from
the fires below; here and there jets of lava sprang hundreds
of feet into the air and burst into rocket-sprays that re-
turned to earth in a crimson rain; and all the while the
laboring mountain shook with Nature's great palsy, and
voiced its distress in moaning and the muffled
booming of subterranean thunders.

—*Mark Twain in Hawaii: Roughing it in the Sandwich Islands,*
Hawaii in the 1860's, 1990.

Kīlauea Volcano, Island of Hawaiʻi

Bromeliad

ONLY IN
Hawai'i

In those days, if a man killed another anywhere on the island the relatives were privileged to take the murderer's life; and then a chase for life and liberty began—the outlawed criminal flying through pathless forests and over mountain and plain, with his hopes fixed upon the protecting walls of the City of Refuge, and the avenger of blood following hotly after him! Sometimes the race was kept up to the very gates of the temple, and the panting pair sped through long files of excited natives, who watched the contest with flashing eye and dilated nostril, encouraging the hunted refugee and sending up a ringing shout of exultation when the saving gates closed upon him and the cheated pursuer sank exhausted at the threshold.

—*Mark Twain in Hawaii: Roughing it in the Sandwich Islands, Hawaii in the 1860's*, 1990.

Pu'uhonua O Honaunau, Island of Hawai'i

Kalo

The first born son of Wakea was of
premature birth and was given the name *Haloa-naka*.
The little thing died, however, and its body was buried in
the ground at one end of the house. After a while from
the child's body shot up a taro plant, the leaf of which was
named *lau-kapa-lili*, quivering leaf; but the stem
was given the name *Haloa*.
After that another child was born to them,
whom they called *Haloa*, from the stalk of the taro. He is
the progenitor of all the peoples of Hawai'i.

—*Native Planters in Old Hawaii: Their Life, Lore, and Environment,* 1972.

Silversword

The Luakini Heiau had many specialized dimensions. A pavement outside of it was known as the kipapa, on which was erected the hale pahu, or house of drums. In the pebbled area would be the paehumu, on which stood an array of wooden images, of which only the moi, or principal one, was sacred. A mana house was set apart for keeping the sacred and all-powerful feathered idol.

—*The Kahuna Sorcerers of Hawaii, Past and Present*, 1979.

Mo'okini Heiau, the Island of Hawai'i

Heliconia

Hibiscus

Lei no Emalani

(Lei Chant for Queen Emma)

I chant this song in praise of my Queen, Answer, beloved Queen, to your lei chant!

The lei-carrier comes from Mo-kau-lele, the bundle-bearer from ʻOhiʻa-ka-lani, the lady with the lei-basket from Kani-ʻahiku.

Puna and Hilo are made seven times more beautiful when bedecked with the finest leis of Wai-akea. Bring these leis and present them to The-Eye-of Ku, Queen Kaumaka who now stands forth in radiance.

She whose leis these are takes them to crown her head, fall from her neck her shoulders.

Kolo-pulepule strung them for her, Wai-luku bore them for her.

May the Queen long so live!

—*The Echo of Our Song, 1973.*

Flower lei

Bibliography

————— *Atlas of Hawaii*. Honolulu: The University of Hawaii Press, 1973.

Cook, Chris, Ed. "Koolau the Leper, A Tragic Love Story." In *A Kaua'i Reader*. Honolulu: Mutual Publishing, 1995.

————— *From the Skies of Paradise: Hawaii*. Honolulu: Mutual Publishing, 1990.

————— "Wai'ale'ale & Beyond." In *A Kaua'i Reader*. Honolulu: Mutual Publishing, 1995.

Day, A. Grove and Carl Stroven, Eds. "The House of the Sun." In *A Hawaiian Reader, Vol I*. Honolulu: Mutual Publishing, 1968.

————— "Two Hawaiian Households on the Hamakua Coast." In *A Hawaiian Reader, Vol I*. Honolulu: Mutual Publishing, 1968.

————— "Impressions of Honolulu, 1873." In *A Hawaiian Reader, Vol II*. Honolulu: Mutual Publishing, 1968.

Handy, E.S. Craighill, Handy, Elizabeth Green, and Pukui, Mary Kawena, *Native Planters in Old Hawaii: Their Life, Lore, and Environment*. Honolulu: Bishop Museum Press, 1972.

Judd, Henry P. *Hawaiian Proverbs and Riddles*. Honolulu: Bernice P. Bishop Museum, Bulletin 77, 1930.

Pukui, Mary Kawena. *'Olelo No'eau: Hawaiian Proverbs and Poetical Sayings*. Honolulu: Bishop Museum Special Publication No. 71, 1983.

Pukui, Mary Kawena & Korn, L. Alfons, Ed. "Lei Chant for Queen Emma." *The Echo of Our Song*. Honolulu: The University of Hawaii Press, 1973.

Rodman, Julius Scammon. *The Kahuna Sorcerers of Hawaii, Past and Present*. New York: Exposition Press. 1979.

Twain, Mark, *Mark Twain in Hawaii: Roughing it in the Sandwich Islands, Hawaii in the 1860's*. Honolulu: Mutual Publishing, 1990.

Westervelt, William D. *Myths and Legends of Hawai'i*. Honolulu: Mutual Publishing, 1987.

————— "Kauhuhu the Shark of Molokai." In *Myths and Legends of Hawai'i*. Honolulu: Mutual Publishing, 1987.